KINGDOM PROMISES
DEVOTIONS EMBRACING FAITH

BUT GOD

KEN HEMPHILL

BROADMAN
& HOLMAN
PUBLISHERS

NASHVILLE, TENNESSEE

KINGDOM PROMISES: **BUT GOD**

ISBN 10: 0-8054-2782-1
ISBN 13: 978-0-8054-2782-0

Broadman & Holman Publishers
Nashville, Tennessee
www.broadmanholman.com

Unless otherwise noted, all Scripture quotations
have been taken from the *Holman Christian Standard
Bible*® Copyright © 1999, 2000, 2002, 2003 by
Holman Bible Publishers.

Other Scriptures used include the New American
Standard Bible (NASB) and the New International
Version (NIV).

Dewey Decimal Classification: 242.5
Devotional Literature / Faith
Printed in the United States
2 3 4   09 08 07 06

I dedicate this book to my wife Paula's brother and his wife:

{ Keith and Beth Moore }

Keith and Beth's passion for youth and their love for God's creation has led them to an effective camping ministry. They have constantly demonstrated "But God" can work through every circumstance.

PREFACE

Studying God's Word always brings its own rewards. I have been deeply moved by these statements scattered throughout the Word of God. It is my prayer that they will minister in your life as they have mine.

As always, I am indebted to my wife, who is my partner in ministry and my encourager in this ministry of writing. She brings the order and solitude to our home that makes it possible for me to reflect and write. She is often the source of ideas that soon appear in my books. Our devotional times together frequently become theological discussions which enrich my understanding.

My children are a constant joy to me, and our growing family provides a rich context for writing. Tina and Brett have been blessed with a daughter, Lois, who is as active as her "papa." Rachael and Trey were blessed with a daughter, Emerson, whose smile lights up a room. It is a joy to watch Katie and Daniel grow in marital love and in the Lord. My family is the context for my entire ministry.

I want to thank Morris Chapman, the visionary leader of the Southern Baptist Convention for calling our denomination to focus on God's Kingdom. He has given me the freedom to write those things God lays on my heart. All of my colleagues at the Executive Committee of the Southern Baptist Convention have encouraged me in this new phase of ministry.

I want to thank Karolyn Chapman, a dear friend in Christ, who challenged me to look for the phrase "But God" in the Scripture. I am honored that she was willing to write a foreword. She and her husband, Gary Chapman, have been great encouragers for Paula and me.

I also want to thank Mary Katherine McClendon, who as a busy student at Southwestern Seminary provided much of the background research for this book. We discovered that God had serendipitously led us both to the same study.

As usual the good folks at Broadman and Holman have been my partners in this ministry. I am challenged by the trust they place in me. Ken Stephens has led Broadman and Holman with integrity of heart.

I can't begin to express my gratitude to Lawrence Kimbrough, my partner in this writing adventure. Lawrence is far more than an editor. He is a friend, colleague, and artist. What he does with a rough draft is a thing of beauty.

This book is somewhat of a new genre. It looks like a daily devotional in its format, but it is written to be "bite-sized" theology. I have attempted to explain each of these great promises in its original context and then to apply it to life. Thus, I highly recommend that you read this book with your Bible open, because the focal passages will have the greatest impact on you as you see them in context. You might also want to consider using these verses as a Scripture memory project while you're reading.

I pray God will use His Word to bring encouragement to your heart. And if this book of Kingdom Promises speaks life to you and ministers to your needs, I hope you'll pass it along to someone else.

Ken Hemphill
Nashville, Tennessee
Spring 2006

FOREWORD

The whole idea of "but God" is amazing to me! This life we know is all because the very God of the universe, the Father of time and creation, set it in motion with reason, with purpose, and with plan.

The writing in this book is practical and simple but very profound – just think about it. As Dr. Hemphill writes, "The center of history is a 'but God'! 'But God raised Him from the dead'." In another chapter he reminds us, "The battle is not yours, but God's." Thus, the idea of trust.

Read well, think well, and enjoy the full meaning of each 'but God'. Thank you, my friend Ken, for taking the challenge and doing such a superb job!

Karolyn Chapman, popular conference speaker, wife of author Gary Chapman

BUT GOD
Steps Into Our Situation

> **Genesis 20:3** But God came to Abimelech in a dream by night.

Have you ever found yourself on the verge of spiritual victory only to be defeated by a familiar enemy? If so, you may identify with this story, rejoicing in the assurance of God's protective care.

Abraham had been steadily learning to trust God as the provision for his life. But even after the moving story of Abraham's intercession for Sodom, when he pled for the city's survival (if only ten righteous people, his nephew Lot among them, could be found there), we are disappointed to find very soon thereafter that he resorted to faithless scheming. While traveling through the Negev and settling between Kadesh and Shur, he tried passing off his wife, Sarah, as his sister.

Abraham explained his action: "I thought, 'There is absolutely no fear of God in this place. They will kill me because of my wife'" (v. 11). Further, he attempted to rationalize his action by claiming that she really was his sister—sort of—the daughter of his father (v. 12). Once again, however, we are reminded of God's grace in the everyday affairs of men. "But God came to Abimelech [the local king] in a dream," setting into motion a series of events that spared Abraham from paying as dearly as he could for his folly.

I find it helpful to read stories like this. They are not glamorous and do not paint Abraham in a very good light, but they are honest. Like Abraham, we often find ourselves falling back into familiar patterns of bad behavior that have been our crutches in the past—even after times of great spiritual victory and advance.

This story should remind us that God is our ultimate and only protection. How arrogant of Abraham to think that his half-truth would provide greater safety for him and his family than the sovereign God of the universe could. When you are tempted to rely on your own ingenuity, remember that God's power is not lessened by the circumstances in which you are living. His Word can always be trusted.

BUT GOD
Knows the True Story

> **Genesis 31:42** But God has
> seen my affliction and my
> hard work.

Have you ever felt like you were
unappreciated at work? Worse yet, have
you ever felt cheated and deceived by your
employer? I suppose all of us have known
people to take advantage of us. They
overlooked what we had done and failed to
give us the credit we deserved. This story
from the life of Jacob will assure you that
these things don't go unnoticed by God.

Jacob had been sent by his father,
Isaac, to Laban's house to find a bride,
since it was inappropriate for him to take a
wife from the Canaanite women. But from
the very beginning Laban had been deceit-
ful in his dealings with Jacob. He first
deceived him concerning his wife and
continually deceived him about his wages.

So one day Jacob left . . . without
telling Laban. He not only took his 401k,
consisting of a considerable flock, but he
also took his two wives, Rachel and Leah,

and all of Laban's grandkids. Jacob was unaware, though, that Rachel had stolen her father's household idol, making matters even worse. So Laban pursued and eventually overtook Jacob. One can imagine he was not intending to give him the proverbial gold watch for twenty years of faithful labor!

But when it came time for the big showdown, Jacob declared that God had seen his affliction and his hard labor. He knew, in fact, that God had come to Laban in a dream the night before, warning him to back off from accusing Jacob. So Laban suggested that they make a covenant between them. They had a meal together. Laban kissed his grandsons and his daughters, blessed them, and left.

Jacob could not have known that God would visit with Laban and defend Jacob's honor in such dramatic fashion. He did understand, however, that God knew his situation and would make things right. We should all pray daily for the eyes to see that God is always at work, and that it is enough to know that he is aware of what we've done and what we're going through.

BUT GOD
Places Us Where He Wants Us

> **Genesis 45:8** It was not you who sent me here, but God.

Seven years of plenty had been followed by seven years of famine, and Jacob and his entire family had been placed at risk by the drought. So when he learned that there was grain to be had in Egypt, he commissioned his sons to go buy some to ensure their family's survival.

We know, of course, that there was more going on in this story than just a business transaction. Jacob's favored son, Joseph, who was thought to have been killed years earlier by a wild animal, had actually been sold to slave traders by his brothers. In fact, Joseph himself was the mastermind who had developed this whole strategy of storing grain during the time of plenty so that Egypt could sell grain to needy nations and people . . . like Jacob.

You remember well the rest of the story—how a silver cup was placed along with the grain in the youngest son's sack, how the brothers were accused of theft, and how Judah pled with Joseph to remain behind as a hostage in Benjamin's place.

But seeing the change in the attitude of his brothers, Joseph revealed to them his identity. In his famous speech to them, the phrases "not you" and "but God" pointed out the Lord's overarching providence in caring for his people. Yes, his brothers had *sold* him, but God had *sent* him. It was God himself who was truly behind the event that had turned his life around.

Here we see the biblical view which somehow incorporates the free will of man with the sovereign provision of God. He is not the cause of evil, but neither is his sovereign design thwarted by our failings. His will is accomplished even in the midst of sin and mistakes.

I find this promise wonderfully comforting. I serve a God who can indeed work together in all circumstances to accomplish his purpose and conform me to his image (Rom. 8:28–29). When you encounter the phrase " but God," be assured that God is always at work.

BUT GOD
Brings Us Out of Bondage

> **Deuteronomy 6:21** We were slaves of Pharaoh in Egypt, but the Lord brought us out of Egypt with a strong hand.

Children have a penchant for asking questions. *Why is the sky blue? If the world spins on its axis, why don't we fall off?* Sometimes we can be busy and think the questions are a wearisome annoyance. But questions provide a wonderful opportunity for the teaching and learning process that is a natural part of growing up.

What do you do when your children ask questions about your family's Christian faith and practice? *Why do we go to church all the time when our neighbors head to the beach on Sunday? Why can't I dress like all the other kids at school?* These questions give the kingdom focused parent a chance to communicate vital truths about God's Word.

Moses understood that the Hebrew children were bound to ask their parents why their lifestyle was in such contrast to the pagans among whom they lived and traveled. This prompted Moses to tell

Israel's moms and dads that an appropriate way to respond to their children's questions would be to remind them of God's redemptive activity in bringing them out of bondage and into the land of promise.

The short statement that reads—"We were slaves . . . but the Lord brought us out"—is indeed a powerful testimony for children to hear.

My father died of a brain tumor several years ago, living only about a year after his initial surgery. During that time, however, God gave him good health and a sound memory. One day we loaded mom and dad and our children into the van and took a trip down memory lane. We went to some of the churches in the Burke County, North Carolina, area where mom and dad grew up. At each stop my parents would tell of the activity of the Lord in their lives. This was one of the precious treasures they left their children and grandchildren.

Have you ever told your children about your redemptive history? You may take it for granted that your children know your story, but tell it to them over and over until they know it is the substance of your life.

BUT GOD
Has a Better Plan

> **Judges 7:4 (NIV)** But the Lord said to Gideon, "There are still too many men."

Judges 6 alerts us to an all too familiar scene for the Israelites. The Midianites and their allies were ready to cross the Jordan and invade a particularly fertile area of land, and there did not appear to be a whole lot Israel could do to prevent this annual foray. But this year would be a different story.

The Bible says the Spirit of the Lord had "enveloped" Gideon, a timid young man from an inconsequential Hebrew family, fully strengthening him for the task at hand. Being so empowered—even though still struggling with his own fear and doubt—Gideon was called out by God to summon the tribes for battle.

But now we encounter the "But God" phrase. And it was a statement that certainly surprised Gideon. God told him that he had too many to go to war with. To obey and agree with this assessment meant going back into the Israelite camp and saying, "I have a great idea—let's get rid of most of our soldiers and go to battle with only a handful!"

It sounded like a plan assured of certain, stunning defeat. The soldiers of Midian, accompanied by the forces of the Amalekites and Qedemites, were so numerous that they looked like a swarm of locusts, and their camels were as innumerable as the sand on the seashore. (Let's hope our band of 300 soldiers performs like comic book superheroes!)

The moral of this story, of course, is that spiritual victory is not based on numbers or human strength. It is based on the presence of the Lord. God wants us to rely on him and not our own strength and ingenuity. By reducing the army to 300 dedicated men, God ensured that the glory would be all his. Because when God receives glory, he draws the nations to himself.

God wants to give you spiritual victory, too, so that you can declare along with the psalmist: "Not to us, Lord, not to us, but to Your name give glory." (Ps. 115:1).

BUT GOD
Sees Our Hearts

{ **1 Samuel 16:7** Man does not
see what the Lord sees, for
man sees what is visible, but
the Lord sees the heart. }

"You can't tell a book by its cover."

"Big gifts come in small packages."

Both sayings communicate a similar
sentiment. We are often guilty of making
superficial judgments based on appearance.
We make snap judgments about people
based on their size, looks, clothes, or
address. And we're certainly not the first
ones in history to do it.

God had rejected Saul as king and had
commissioned Samuel to anoint the next
king of Israel. So God instructed him to go
to a man named Jesse in Bethlehem, being
simply told, "You are to anoint for Me the
one I indicate to you" (1 Sam. 16:3).

Samuel began the search for the next
king with the use of his own insight. Eliab,
Jesse's firstborn, came before Samuel. He
was immediately impressed with Eliab's
appearance and stature. He thus conclud-
ed: "Certainly the Lord's anointed one is

here before Him" (16:6). He was, after all, the firstborn son and apparently had the look of a king.

But before a single drop of anointing oil could spill onto Eliab's head, the Lord made it clear to Samuel that he did not see things in the same perspective that man does. The Lord looks at the size and purity of a man's heart over the size of his body and his physical appeal.

Jesse then called his other sons in consecutive order, and all were rejected. It puzzled Samuel that God had not chosen any of the sons that had been paraded past him. He then asked, "Are these all the sons you have?" (16:11). Yes, there was one—the youngest—but he was tending the sheep. Could the least of all be the one chosen by God for greatness?

It is important to remember that God is looking for servants with a big heart. You may not think you are kingdom quality. None of your friends may have selected you for greatness. David's father didn't even invite him to the sacrifice. But when you have been selected by the King of the universe, that should be enough.

BUT GOD
Protects Us

> **1 Samuel 23:14** Saul searched
> for him every day, but God did
> not hand David over to him.

Have you ever felt like someone was
out to get you? Have you had that uneasy
feeling that there is something or someone
lurking out there who desires to do you
harm? We can learn a lesson from a great
man of the Bible who had an adversary like
that who "searched for him every day."

Saul was still the titular king of Israel,
but his days were numbered because he
had disobeyed God's instructions and had
become arrogant in his own achievement,
even going so far as to set up a monument
to himself. Samuel, then, was given the
difficult assignment of telling Saul that God
had rejected him. David would become
king in Saul's place.

From the very beginning we see a
totally different attitude and spirit in David
than in Saul as he willingly served the very
king he was destined to replace. When
Saul was tormented by an evil spirit, David

played his harp to comfort him. When Saul was frightened by the giant Goliath, David defeated the Philistine who dared defy the army of the Lord. But David's success only served to breed greater hatred in the heart of Saul, who began an all-out campaign to kill David.

As this threat became more overt and obvious, David refused to respond in kind. He had several opportunities to take Saul's life but refused to lay a hand on him. His strategy was simple but clear—stay away from Saul! He took steps calculated to provide protection, moving from place to place, seeking out remote, desert areas and easily defensible places—"in the wilderness strongholds and in the hill country" (1 Sam. 23:14).

The key to David's protection, however, was not his own ingenuity. He understood that the Lord was his protection, and therefore we are told, *"But God* did not hand David over to him."

We can take every precaution to avoid conflict with those who would harm us. But the Lord is our true protector, and he will do the hard work of keeping us safe.

BUT GOD
Does Not Banish Us

> **2 Samuel 14:14** But God would not take away a life . . . so that the one banished from Him does not remain banished.

While God forgives sin, we must never forget that sin always leaves scars. Even David's family, we know, was fractured by sin. Bathsheba's son died, David's son Amnon raped his sister Tamar, and Absalom in turn murdered Amnon for disgracing her. Absalom then fled from his father, for he knew that the Torah would require his death.

David became increasingly distraught over this. Even his nephew Joab, commander of the Israelite forces, "observed that the king's mind was on Absalom" constantly (2 Sam. 14:1).

So Joab concocted a rather creative plan to convince David to pardon his son. He enlisted the help of a wise woman from Tekoa, who costumed herself as a woman in mourning. She made up the story that one of her sons had killed the other while they were alone in the field, and she came to David on the pretense of pleading for her son's life. Even though the law required the son's death (Exod. 21:12), David chose to spare him, much as God had allowed Cain to live after killing Abel.

Having solved the woman's problem, David expected her to leave, but she boldly asked to speak a word to the king. He graciously granted it, and the real drama began. She appealed to David to pardon his own banished son, too—Absalom. She then cited a truth based on God's warnings to Adam and Eve in the garden: "we will certainly die and be like water poured out on the ground" (14:14). Then came the profound "But God" truth: even though life is such that it requires death, God works to combat death and spare life.

This story provides a wonderful picture of the gospel. God has himself provided a way "that the one banished from Him does not remain banished." It is true that all have sinned and deserve death, but Jesus died in our place that we might not be forever banished from the Lord, now or ever.

What a great kingdom promise!

BUT GOD
Is Our Support

2 Samuel 22:19 They confronted me in the day of my distress, but the Lord was my support.

Do you ever feel overwhelmed? Do the odds seem to be stacked against you? Do you sometimes fall into despair and wonder if you can get through another day? Guess what? You are in good company. This "But God" saying comes from the great King David and is found in the longest quotation attributed to him in the book of Samuel.

If you were to read the chapters preceding this, you would get an appreciation for the note of celebration in this text. You may recall that David had experienced family tumult because of his sin with Bathsheba. And while preoccupied with all of this family pressure, a wicked man named Sheba fomented rebellion against David, encouraging the men of Israel to desert him. Next we are told that a three-year famine covered the land. Enough already, right? Not quite! David was then forced to go to battle against the Philistine giants. The end of 21:15 tells it all—"But David became exhausted."

I find it fascinating that David's "but" statement is followed by, "But the Lord was my support." This great hymn of praise contains some of our favorite statements about God's power. "The Lord is my rock, my fortress, and my deliverer, my God, my mountain where I seek refuge, my shield, the horn of my salvation, my stronghold, my refuge, and my Savior." (22:2–3). David pictured the Lord as reaching down and pulling him out of deep waters.

This image of support must have had a special place in David's heart. The word for support can be translated "staff." It is the Hebrew word that refers to a large stick with a bowed top used by shepherds to pull sheep out of danger. David's mighty God is depicted as a caring shepherd who took his staff and snatched David from disaster and delivered him into a spacious place.

When you find that you have more on your plate than you can handle, start to praise the God who is your support. Can you sense the touch of his staff?

BUT GOD
Is Gracious

> **2 Kings 13:23** But the Lord was gracious to them and had compassion on them and turned toward them because of His covenant.

Do you remember as a child when you had done something you knew your parents didn't approve of, and yet no discipline was meted out? You might have been tempted to think your parents didn't know or didn't care. Later, though, you discovered that they had simply been patient with you. They loved you and wanted you to respond to their grace, not just their correction.

Israel was a little slow to learn this.

In verse 1 of 2 Kings 13, we read the headline version of the news—"Jehoahaz son of Jehu became king over Israel in Samaria," where he ruled for seventeen years. So far, so good! The next verse, however, contains the bad news. "He did what was evil in the Lord's sight." Furthermore, he caused all Israel to sin along with him. The indictment was clear and swift. The Lord allowed Israel to receive the consequences of their sin, employing Syria as the instrument of God's discipline. Under normal circumstances they would have destroyed Israel.

The only reason this catastrophe had been delayed was by the grace and compassion of the Lord, based in his faithfulness to his own covenant. Even though Israel deserved to be banished from God's presence for their persistent wickedness, patience flowed from God's character. Yet Israel took God's patience for granted, continued in their wicked ways, and were ultimately taken into captivity by Assyria.

Have you ever taken God's patience for granted? Perhaps you know that you are tolerating sin in your own life, and yet God has not yet brought judgment. Rather than thanking God for his patience and kindness, you may have behaved as if holy God is unconcerned or unaware of your sin.

When we experience God's patience with us as frail children, our response should be to turn from our sin and allow him to fully restore our relationship. We should live every day in grateful thanks for God's gracious compassion.

BUT GOD
Is Our Creator

> **1 Chronicles 16:26** All the
> gods of the people are idols,
> but the Lord made the heavens.

David had just been installed as
king of Israel. And one of his first acts
of leadership was to return the ark of the
covenant to Jerusalem. It was quite an
affair. David assembled singers who were
to raise their voices with joy, accompanied
by musical instruments—harps, lyres, and
cymbals. What a scene as all of Israel,
decked out in their finest, paraded and
processed with the ark of God's presence.

In this context we find one of the most
powerful hymns of thanksgiving contained
in all the Bible. The readers (or listeners in
David's day) were exhorted to give thanks,
to call on God's name, to publicize his
deeds among the peoples, to sing praise
and give him honor. All of this was a grand
reminder to the people of God's faithfulness to his covenant.

The theme changes a bit in verse 23 of
this chapter, however, when the kingship of

the Lord is underlined, as well as the universal implications of his rule. "Sing to the Lord, all the earth. Proclaim His salvation from day to day. Declare His glory among the nations, His wonderful works among all peoples" (vv. 23–24).

What is the basis of this admonition to declare his glory among the nations and peoples? The "But God" promise puts it all in perspective. The God of Israel is not one God among many. All other gods are but idols that are created by the ingenuity of man. "But the Lord made the heavens!" That says it all.

Have you ever wondered why the Bible talks so often about the creation of the heavens and the earth? Creation is not a minor doctrine confined to the first few chapters of Genesis. It is a bedrock truth. God is King of all the earth and its people groups because he is their creator. He desires to be their redeemer, and therefore he calls people to himself to become the means by which he is declared among all peoples.

Have you told anyone lately about your love relationship with the King?

BUT GOD
Will Do Your Fighting

> **2 Chronicles 20:15** Do not
> be afraid or discouraged . . .
> for the battle is not yours,
> but God's.

Have you ever looked at your circumstances and sighed, "If the Lord doesn't
provide a miracle, I'm sunk"? Guess what,
you have something in common with an
ancient king named Jehoshaphat.

This chapter opens with a somber
warning—that a vast multitude of armies,
consisting of some of the day's most threat-
ening and deadly nations, had marshaled
their armies against Israel.

Jehoshaphat's first reaction was fear,
an altogether reasonable response given the
circumstances. It is not wrong to be afraid.
The question is how we respond to our
fear. Notice, then, the second response of
Jehoshaphat: he resolved to seek the Lord.
This mighty king called the people to pray
and also led them in prayer. Jehoshaphat
knew how to deal with his fear.

His prayer is worthy of our attention.
"Lord God of our ancestors, are You not

the God who is in heaven, and do You not rule over all the kingdoms of the nations? Power and might are in Your hand, and no one can stand against You" (20:6). Notice that Jehoshaphat didn't focus on his dire circumstances but on the power and majesty of God. Listen to his confidence: "We will cry out to You because of our distress, and You will hear and deliver" (v. 9). I love both his honesty and his tenacity: "We do not know what to do, but we look to You" (v. 12).

Once the king and the people had brought their petition before the Lord, they stood patiently before him. Jahaziel, a Levite who could trace his lineage back to the psalmist Asaph, was inspired to give God's divine response. He began and ended with the same emphasis—"Do not be afraid or discouraged."

The counsel "do not fear" occurs 365 times in the Bible, as one commentator reports, giving us one for every day of the year. This is a convincing number of times to remind us why we can take courage. We do not face our enemies alone. The battle is not ours but God's.

BUT GOD
Surrounds Us with His Love

> **Psalm 32:10** Many pains come to the wicked, but the one who trusts in the Lord will have faithful love surrounding him.

We know that "many pains come to the wicked." Not only have we seen this in others, we have experienced the reality in ourselves. We know that our thoughts, our motives, and our feelings often betray our desire to be holy as our Father is holy.

The "but" statement that arrests our attention does not say "but God," as in many of the others we have studied. Nonetheless this verse refers to the covenant loyalty of a God who demonstrates faithful love to those who trust in him. What an incredible promise! Would you like to feel his love enfold you like a warm comforter on a cold night?

If so, pay close attention to the context of this promise. Psalm 32 is about the joy of forgiveness. "How happy is the one whose transgression is forgiven, whose sin is covered!" (v. 1). But how about those who continue in sin, ignoring its hold on them?

"When I kept silent, my bones became brittle from my groaning all day long" (v. 3), draining his strength as in summer's heat.

Given the option, then, of the joy of forgiveness or the pain of concealed sin, which would you choose? The psalmist chose to acknowledge and confess his sin. And because of the freedom he enjoyed from being forgiven, he could declare, "You are my hiding place; You protect me from trouble. You surround me with joyful shouts of deliverance" (v. 7).

So how do we experience this enfolding love? The psalmist has a simple yet profound answer. "Do not be like a horse or mule, without understanding . . . or else it will not come near you" (v. 9). The stubborn animal must be controlled with bit and bridle. But not the one who trusts in the Lord. He is led in God's faithful love.

You have two options today. Ignore your sin and experience the pain of the wicked, or acknowledge your sin and be surrounded by faithful love. When we come to God in our weakness, he surrounds us with his strength.

BUT GOD
Delivers Us from Trouble

> **Psalm 34:19** Many adversities come to the one who is righteous, but the Lord delivers him from them all.

It is easier to celebrate the last half of this promise than accept the reality of the first half. We like to be delivered, but we don't like to face adversity. I'm not suggesting, of course, that you should go looking for trouble. But don't worry; you won't have to. If you choose to be righteous—to live in a right relationship with God—adversity will find you. Righteous living goes against the grain of our culture, creating a certain friction which can lead to adversity.

This psalm actually tells us the occasion in David's life which prompted these words and this promise. The story is found in 1 Samuel 21:10–15, when David was fleeing for his life, forced to act like a madman in order to survive. And though he was humbled by the encounter, he nonetheless praised God for it: "I will praise the Lord at all times; His praise will always be on my lips" (v. 1). Praise is the gateway to deliverance. If you are trapped by discouragement or despair, praise the Lord anyway.

Truly, when we focus on the Lord's greatness, we will begin to seek him. And that's when we discover that "the eyes of the Lord are on the righteous, and His ears are open to their cry for help" (v. 15).

When I read this verse, I am reminded of the little boy who was afraid of the dark. When his dad would turn out the light in his son's bedroom, the boy's only question was, "Which way is your face turned?" Even though the boy's eyes could not penetrate the darkness, he was comforted by the knowledge that his father's face was toward him.

While the Bible offers no glib guarantees that we will escape crises and trials, God does promise that we can count on his presence and deliverance. Verse 20, in fact, includes the messianic prophecy that "he protects all his bones; not one of them is broken," referring to Christ's death on the cross. Yes, we have resurrected proof that God delivers the righteous!

BUT GOD
Repels Our Enemies

> **Psalm 64:6–7** They . . . say, "We have perfected a secret plan". . . but God will shoot them with arrows.

This is a wonderful promise about God's righteous judgment of sin and his desire to protect his children from evildoers. But to fully appreciate it, we need to look at the entire passage.

Note how Psalm 64 begins—with a simple yet important request. The psalmist asked the Lord to hear him and deliver him from the terror or dread of the enemy. The emotion spoken of is one of paralyzing fear, a state of mind that would keep him from thinking clearly and taking positive action.

Perhaps you can identify with this. What or who is it that terrorizes you? Have you asked the Lord to deliver you from your dread?

After this the psalmist turned to the enemy's strategy. The terms he used tell us that his adversary had no intention of fighting fairly. He spoke of the "scheming of the wicked" and "the mob of evildoers"

(v. 2). Those who would destroy us, he said, "sharpen their tongues like swords and aim bitter words like arrows" (v. 3). They attack without warning from "concealed places" (v. 4). They "encourage each other" in their evil scheming (v. 5). When they devise a plan, they declare it to be perfect (v. 6). Sound familiar? I am sure you've met this kind of enemy before.

The solution for turning back the assault, however, is swift and appropriate—"But God will shoot them with arrows." Yes, our adversary is defeated by his own weapons. When I read this verse I am reminded of the biblical truth that we will reap what we sow.

So the request from verse 1—to be delivered from dread—is more than abundantly answered by the promise of God's action. Judgment may not occur until sometime in the future, but it is certain and it will be swift. Therefore, we can begin to rejoice now and "take refuge" in the Lord (v. 10).

Our vision is limited and we often despair when we see the unrighteous prosper. Remember—But God!

BUT GOD
Listens to Our Prayer

> **Psalm 66:19** However,
> God has listened; He has
> paid attention to the sound
> of my prayer.

Paula and I have been married for most of our lives, yet we sometimes fail to communicate effectively. We frequently find ourselves saying, "You don't listen!" It's true. I often find myself hearing but not really listening. How frustrating to make an effort to communicate, only to discover that the one to whom you're speaking just isn't listening.

But I have good news: God listens!

Psalm 66 tells us two important things about the effective practice of prayer. First, the psalm magnifies the priority of praise. "I cried out to Him with my mouth, and praise was on my tongue" (v. 17). Even in times of deep distress (v. 14), we should begin our prayers with praise.

Praise is always an appropriate response for the privilege of entering into the presence of the King. Our prayers are punctuated with praise because God is worthy of praise. He inhabits the praise of his people, and thus praise makes us more acutely aware of his presence.

Second, this psalm underlines the importance of absolute sincerity. "If I had been aware of malice in my heart, the Lord would not have listened" (v. 18). David understood that it was important to enter into the presence of holy God with a pure heart, having lived in obedience, having done what he had promised.

Early in the taking of the Promised Land, Israel suffered an unexpected defeat at Ai. Some of the Israelites had taken the spoils of war, which had been forbidden by the Lord. So God ordered them to come before him tribe by tribe and remove that which had been taken in disobedience. This is sort of what our confession should be like as we talk with our Father.

But David doesn't simply rejoice in the fact that God has answered his prayer, but that he is a God who listens. "He has not turned away my prayer or turned His faithful love from me" (v. 20). Prayer is an indication of unbroken relationship with God—proof that he is listening.

BUT GOD
Is Our Strength

> **Psalm 73:26** My flesh and my heart may fail, but God is the strength of my heart, my portion forever.

Have you ever been envious of the prosperity of the wicked? Do you ever wonder why those who cut corners seem to get all the breaks in life? If you had to answer "yes"—and who wouldn't?—you are in pretty good company. When the psalmist Asaph looked at the wicked, he noted that they have an easy time, their bodies are well-fed, they are not in trouble, and they are not "afflicted like most people" (vv. 4–5). They mock God and appear to get away with it.

The bottom line is clearly stated in verse 12: "Look at them—the wicked! They are always at ease, and they increase their wealth." Just to look at them, you'd think they had everything in the world a person could possibly want.

Does this description bring anyone to mind? Do you sometimes find that you too are envious of those who have all the stuff you can't afford and can't attain? What is the solution?

We can see the beginning of victory in verses 16–17. "When I tried to understand all this, it seemed hopeless until I entered God's sanctuary. Then I understood their destiny." The light came on when Asaph turned to the Lord in worship. There he discovered the eternal contrast—that those who live for themselves with no regard for God are certain to fall into ultimate and eternal ruin.

So how foolish of us to be bitter and envious toward the wicked, when we are being held even now by the hand of God and are assured of one day being taken up to glory (vv. 23–24). What else could we really want? A relationship with God is more than enough.

In the meantime, yes, our "heart" may feel low and discouraged. Certainly at some point, our physical "flesh" will die. But no matter—God is both the "strength" of our heart and our "portion" forever, both the power for present day living and the promise of our eternal inheritance.

Why, then, should we envy anyone?

BUT GOD
Purifies Our Hearts

> **Proverbs 17:3** A crucible is for silver and a smelter for gold, but the Lord is a tester of hearts.

Have you ever seen someone refine silver or gold? It is fascinating to watch as the heat is applied and the impurities rise to the surface so they can be removed. This smelting process is necessary, of course, to purify the metal and reduce it to its most valuable state.

But while it's easy to talk theoretically about the smelting process of the soul, it is much more difficult to accept it when it is practically applied to our lives.

If we only looked at the second half of this proverb, we might be led to conclude that God was nothing more than a cosmic examiner, a heartless "tester of hearts." The first line, however, suggests that God's desire is a constructive one—to remove the dross from our lives so that we may be more productive.

Peter used this same picture of refining in 1 Peter 1:6–7, when he spoke of God's reasoning behind the various trials we encounter: "so that the genuineness of your faith—more valuable than gold, which perishes though refined by fire—may result in praise, glory, and honor at the revelation of Jesus Christ."

This benefit is not always automatic, however, depending on how God's purging is received. Jeremiah spoke of a refining process where the bellows blow but the refining is completely in vain. "They are called rejected silver, for the Lord has rejected them" (Jer. 6:30). Those rejected are described as stubborn rebels.

Ask yourself, then—how do you respond to God's refining fire? It may come in the various trials of life. It may be that God refines us through disappointment, failure, or suffering. Do you trust the hand of God in these trials and look for him to work his purpose for your good in everything? Or do you rebel and blame God for being unfair?

In every circumstance we should ask God to refine us so that our very lives will advance his kingdom, by his power, for his glory. May his look inside our hearts give him pleasure.

BUT GOD
Judges Our Motives

> **Proverbs 21:2** All the ways of a man seem right to him, but the Lord evaluates the motives.

There is a famous line that says everyone in prison considers themselves to be innocent. We are all good at rationalizing our own failures. In fact, some years ago I read about a popular musician who blamed his drug problem and all his other dysfunctions on his fans. He said the pressure they exerted on him to be at his best caused him to cope in destructive ways. Talk about putting the blame anywhere but where it belongs!

But before we become too glib in talking about criminals and popular musicians, we must bring this proverb home. All of us manage to talk ourselves into doing what we want to do, convincing ourselves that what we did was right given the circumstances.

But herein lies the danger of basing our behavior on our own feelings: we can deceive ourselves. "All the ways of a man seem right to him." When we set our own standard for a passing grade, we will always pass. The rub comes, however, when we realize that our actions and motives will be judged against a standard of righteousness established by a holy God. Then we come to the stark realization that our rationalization is dangerous.

God is not fooled by our pretenses. He judges our motives. Although we make many judgments based on outward appearance, God is able to discern the very intent of our hearts. (By the way, you will find this proverb in essentially the same form in 16:2. It seems likely that the Holy Spirit wanted to make sure we got the message.)

How, then, can we guard our hearts from this kind of self-deceit? I think the writer of Hebrews gave us the best solution. "For the word of God is living and effective and sharper than any two-edged sword, penetrating as far as to divide soul, spirit, joints, and marrow; it is a judge of the ideas and thoughts of the heart" (4:12). Stay in God's Word and allow it to bring you into conformity with God's standard of righteousness.

BUT GOD
Knows His Plans for Us

> **Jeremiah 1:7 (NASB)** But the
> Lord said to me, "Do not say, 'I
> am a youth,' because every-
> where I send you, you shall go.

Have you ever argued with God about
your lack of ability? Suppose he prompts
you to talk to a friend about the gospel, but
you excuse yourself because it's not natural
for you to talk openly about spiritual
things. Someone in your church asks you
to teach a class or sing a solo, and you
humbly reply that you're too shy, too
young, too scared. You get the idea!

But whenever you argue with your
Creator—the sovereign God of the universe—you are destined to lose, because
God has a design and purpose for your life,
and it is only in that purpose that you will
find fulfillment.

Jeremiah discovered this. One of the
best known and most autobiographical of
the Old Testament prophets, he invited
readers into his very thoughts as he strug-
gled with the task God had assigned him.
In fact, as we begin to read the book of

Jeremiah, we are allowed to overhear a dialogue in which God tells him that even before Jeremiah was conceived in the womb, God had a purpose for him: to be God's spokesman to the nations in a chaotic time and to deliver a most unpopular message, one of impending judgment on Israel for their disobedience.

Jeremiah responded to this commission with a disclaimer and an excuse, declaring that he was no speaker, and that he was too young to accept such a task.

But the simplicity of God's response indicates that he never makes a mistake in choosing his servants. He empowers us. He dwells within us. He protects us and equips us to accomplish our God-given purpose.

And while God may not have called you to be a prophet to the nations, he has indeed created you with kingdom purpose. "For we are His creation — created in Christ Jesus for good works, which God prepared ahead of time so that we should walk in them" (Eph. 2:10).

Yes, God has already planned the good works you will accomplish for him. Even now, you can see him at work in you.

BUT GOD
Is the One True God

> **Jeremiah 10:10** But the Lord is the true God; He is the living God and eternal King.

I was walking through my side yard in Virginia Beach when a pungent yet sweet odor caught my attention. Soon a strange melody in a foreign tongue joined with the fragrance to stop me in my tracks. I could see my new neighbor through her open window as she knelt before a homemade altar praying to her god, a simple idol made of clay.

I was stunned. This was Virginia Beach, not Bangladesh. Yet as I reflected on this idol worship next door to me, I began to see idol worship all around. Some of the idols took the form of boats and jet skis. Others were more subtle and didn't have an obvious form. They were lodges, clubs, and ball teams that held the affection of my neighbors and drew their attention and devotion from the one true God.

The first part of Jeremiah 10 describes this contrast, speaking so logically to make the point undeniably obvious. Idols are created by man, but God created man. Idols are dependent on man, whereas man is dependent on God. They are mute "like scarecrows in a cucumber patch" (v. 5), but God speaks.

To attempt to compare the Creator of the universe with other gods or creatures shows an absolute ignorance of his true character and attributes. God is the true God; idols are false gods. He is living; they are dead. He is eternal; they are transitory. Every word and phrase in verse 10 is filled with theological intent. And these truths continue to be underlined in verses 11 and 12, where we are told that idols will "perish from the earth," whereas God made the earth by his power. Both the power and wisdom of God is clearly manifested in his creation.

Since he alone is truly God, does he have your total worship today? Does anything or anyone draw your passion and devotion away from him? Look at your calendar and checkbook before you answer. Idolatry is a subtle thing. Tell him today that your heart's desire is to serve the one true God.

BUT GOD
Is Our Refuge

> **Joel 3:16** Heaven and earth
> will shake. But the Lord will
> be a refuge for His people.

I was in Florida in late 2004 after the
state had been ravaged by storm after
storm. While there, I remembered back to
news accounts that had reported how, even
with all the hurricane warnings, there had
been people who either couldn't leave or
had chosen not to. As the storms had
raged, many of their houses had been
reduced to rubble.

Yet even in the most devastated areas,
there were a few substantial buildings that
became a haven for those stranded in the
storm. With people's lives in crisis, these
places were their refuge.

Like many Old Testament prophets,
Joel spoke in a time of great crisis. The
immediate crisis was a plague of locusts so
severe that it impacted the harvest for more
than a year. But Joel saw in this invasion
of locusts a picture of an even greater
impending danger—the day of the Lord,

when God would bring severe judgment on his wayward people. Joel's prophecy was intended to be a wake-up call.

The section where our verse is located contains Joel's final reference to the day of the Lord, a great day of judgment that will bring cosmic upheaval. "The sun and moon will grow dark, and the stars will cease their shining" (v. 15). If these stable bodies of the natural world aren't strong enough to be eclipsed by the coming of the Lord, it stands to reason that mere mortals will have little chance of escape. If the roaring winds of a hurricane are frightening, they pale in comparison to the roar of the Lord at his return. The sound of his voice will shake "heaven and earth."

But God is a refuge and a stronghold for his people. This imagery of a place of refuge is similar to that found in Psalm 46:1 — "God is our refuge and strength, a helper who is always found in times of trouble."

I don't know what storm you are facing today, but I can promise you that the God who promised to be Israel's refuge is available to be yours, as well.

BUT GOD
Can Change Our Plans

> **Amos 7:15** But the Lord took me from following the flock and said to me, "Go, prophesy to My people Israel."

Have you ever had a divine interruption? You may think yours doesn't compare with the one Amos recounted, but you may be surprised. The truth is, kingdom people will have regular divine interruptions if they just look and listen.

When we think of Old Testament prophets, we often have a preconceived notion. We tend to regard them as professionals. We might compare them with preachers today. We're partially correct in that assessment, because—yes—there were prophetic guilds in Amos's day.

But he didn't belong to any of them.

If you read the context of our passage, you will discover that Amaziah the priest of Bethel wasn't at all thrilled by the message of Amos, who had been assigned the unenviable task of pronouncing judgment and exile. So Amaziah told Amos to go to Judah and preach for a living there. In response

Amos declared, "I was not a prophet or the son of a prophet" (v. 14). He disavowed any contact with the prophetic guilds of his day. In other words, he had no accredited seminary degree. He was a simple herdsman and dresser of sycamore trees.

Bible teachers debate about the social standing of Amos. His obvious concern for the poor has caused some scholars to conclude he was from the poorer class. Others describe him as a wealthy sheep owner. Whatever the case, he was just a businessman minding his own business when he experienced a divine interruption. "But God" had an extraordinary assignment for an ordinary man.

Do you expect God to interrupt your day? If you will simply look and listen, he will. God has daily and regular assignments for all his kingdom people. Ask him today to show you where he is working around you. Ask him to give you the ears to hear his voice when he interrupts you while you are just minding your ordinary business. Every day is full of kingdom opportunity if you will give the Lord the permission to interrupt you.

BUT GOD
Is Over All

We know nothing about Habakkuk apart from this brief book bearing his name. His message was set against the backdrop of the decline and fall of the kingdom of Judah, a period in which they enjoyed a last gasp of hope under the good king Josiah. But conditions spiraled from prosperity and the hope of revival to the pit of desperation as the net of destruction was drawn around Judah.

Habakkuk's prophecy, as one might anticipate by the historical setting, was marked by a series of "woes." In this particular section the prophet declared: "Woe to him who says to wood: Wake up!" (2:19), underlining the obvious futility of trusting in idols created by mere man.

The contrast between unloving idols and the living God couldn't be stated more powerfully or eloquently. "But the Lord is in His holy temple; let everyone on earth be silent in His presence." This simple statement assures us that our God is a living God, ruling and judging in sovereign power, worthy of our humble submission and reverent trust.

When everything around you that was once nailed down seems to be coming loose, how do you respond? Do you come before him in silent adoration with absolute confidence that he is at work in everything for your good, or do you turn to vain idols made of wood or stone?

I know this idolatry thing is a little hard to grasp, but it is more subtle than we think. We reflect the same mentality as the idolaters when we turn to lucky charms, be they crosses or crystals; when we check a daily horoscope . . . just to be sure; when we think anything or anyone controls our destiny other than the living God.

Appropriately, the very next word from the mouth of Habakkuk was a prayer of adoration. "Lord, I have heard the report about You; Lord, I stand in awe of Your deeds. Revive Your work in these years" (3:2). This simple prayer will bring more comfort than all the idols you can amass.

BUT GOD
Forgives Our Sins

> **Luke 5:21** Who is this man who speaks blasphemies? Who can forgive sins but God alone?

Psychologists, sociologists, philosophers, and the rest of us have pondered the questions related to man's sin problem. Some have actually tried to dismiss it altogether, hoping that by denying sin, our problem with it will somehow go away. It doesn't work, though, does it? We know intuitively what the Bible declares unequivocally: "For all have sinned and fall short of the glory of God" (Rom. 3:23).

Perhaps you remember the event surrounding today's "But God" verse. Jesus was teaching and the crowds had gathered to hear him, with the Pharisees and the teachers of the law among them. Several men had brought a paralyzed friend to Jesus for healing. But since the room was packed to capacity, they removed the tiles from the roof and lowered the man into the middle of the crowd. A grand entrance!

Jesus first words were unexpected. "Friend, your sins are forgiven you" (5:20). It would have been less startling if he had said, "Get up and walk." After all, what did a paralyzed man need most? But Jesus' primary purpose was to deliver man from the paralysis of sin that, left unchecked, will ultimately lead to spiritual death.

These words provoked an immediate reaction from the learned theologians. Their first assertion, formed in the guise of a question, was actually correct: "Who can forgive sins but God alone?" But their conclusion was wrong—that Jesus spoke blasphemy when he pronounced forgiveness. They could never understand that Jesus' relationship with God was such that he was indeed able to forgive sin. (In fact, he went on to demonstrate this authority by healing the paralytic's physical illness.)

And so in the end, the man bore the cot that once bore him, but he left with praise on his lips for more than legs that functioned and a body that could walk upright. Who can forgive sin? God alone through his Son, Jesus. Have you experienced the forgiveness of your sin?

BUT GOD
Holds the Future

> **Luke 12:20** But God said to him, "You fool! This very night your life is demanded of you."

Have you ever asked a really inappropriate question at a really bad time? That's the context in which this verse appears.

Jesus was teaching about eternal values, and "someone from the crowd"—without giving any indication that he had heard anything Jesus said—called out, "Teacher, tell my brother to divide the inheritance with me" (v. 13). Talk about inappropriate! Jewish laws of succession covered most cases related to inheritance, but as with any statute, there was sometimes room for doubt. This man's statement suggests that he was regarding Jesus as a typical rabbi who could render opinions on disputed matters of law.

Here's the real tragedy of the story. The man known to us only as "someone" had the opportunity to ask the Son of Man about issues that could impact eternity, yet he chose to ask about a mere temporal matter. Jesus' concern was not to bring wealth to men, but to bring men to eternal wealth.

Characteristically, Jesus used this pregnant moment to teach his hearers about the fatal folly of covetousness. He told a story—a parable—about a wealthy man who had been blessed with a harvest of such magnitude that it created a storage problem.

Here we encounter the "But God" that no one wants to hear. This man had built his entire life without ever considering the fact that the reason God had blessed him was so he could use his wealth wisely— helping others while providing a fuller life for himself. Notice the repeated use of the pronouns "I," "my," and "myself" in his vocabulary. He had made a gross miscalculation by thinking he controlled his own future.

Thus he faced the ultimate question: "The things you have prepared—whose will they be?" (v. 20). Have you honestly faced that question? Kingdom people desire to be rich toward God, using their earthly resources to advance his kingdom.

BUT GOD
Has Made Himself Known

> **John 1:18 (NIV)** No one has ever seen God, but God the One and Only . . . has made him known.

"No one has ever seen God," John the Baptist said.

If you are a student of the Old Testament, you may even now be flipping to Exodus 24:9–11, where we are told that Moses and other leaders of Israel did in fact see God. Even later in Exodus we read that Moses pled with God to allow him to see his glory, which he did—at least from behind.

These Old Testament appearances, including such events as the burning bush and the cloud of glory, are called theophanies. But at best they were partial revelations. Even today, we are able to see something of God in creation and through his mighty works in history. But we cannot see God himself.

If mortal man cannot see or know the essential being of God, what hope is there that we could ever know him personally?

This leads to one of the most beautiful "But God" statements in all of Scripture — "But God . . . has made him known."

You may have noticed that some translations have the word "Son" here, while others have "God." This occurs because early manuscripts slightly differ at this point. But whichever manuscript one selects, the meaning remains unaltered. Christ has made God known to man because all of God's fullness dwells in Christ. He is the "image of the invisible God" (Col. 1:15).

This is the profound miracle and truth of the incarnation: in Jesus, God took upon himself human flesh and dwelt among his creation. This truth is not only profound, it is also exclusive. God cannot be known by man except in Christ; therefore, it is impossible for man to know God apart from His Son. That's why Jesus would later declare: "I am the way, the truth, and the life. No one comes to the Father except through Me" (John 14:6).

So if you are looking for direction, it is Jesus. If you are searching for the truth, it is Jesus. If you desire life, it is Jesus.

BUT GOD
Keeps His Promises

> **Acts 7:5** He didn't give him an inheritance in it . . . but He promised to give it to him as a possession.

Have you ever clung to one of God's promises even though every fiber of rational thought dictated against it? If so, you will find encouragement from this story about Abraham that Stephen mentioned in his address to the members of the Sanhedrin, the powerful ruling authority of the Jews. It reminds us that God doesn't always work on our schedule, but he always fulfills his word.

God called Abraham to leave the familiar territory of his homeland and travel to the place that God would show him. He wasn't given an actual destination, only a promise. This is the way faith works, the way it grows and develops.

We all claim we want to have greater faith. Yet when God gives us the opportunity, we often recoil at the challenge, wanting to wait until we have little more evidence. Abraham, however, simply did as God directed, moving from Haran to Canaan. Yet strangely, he was given no part of the land in actual possession, not even a foot of ground. For the entirety of his life, he dwelled as a resident alien there, clinging only to the promise that his descendants would possess the land. The plot, of course, only intensified, seeing that Abraham was and remained childless for many years. Even after the promised descendants were born, they lived in exile in Egypt for 400 years.

Their exile would not be a permanent one, however. In his own time God would judge the nation that had oppressed them. Israel would again come home to worship him in the land of promise. But Abraham didn't have the hindsight of history to help him make his decisions. He had to believe in God alone and act accordingly.

We, too, must be willing to take the long view of our lives, trusting that God knows what is best, even in those years beyond our own earthly lives. When we have no other evidence than the promise of God, that alone is sufficient, because God is truth and cannot lie.

BUT GOD
Has a Role for Everyone

> **Acts 9:15** But the Lord said to him, "Go! For this man is My chosen instrument."

If we were to conduct a poll about the people who had the greatest impact on first century Christianity, there would be virtual unanimity about the significance of the apostle Paul. But there were lesser known people behind the scenes whom the Lord employed to make it possible for Paul to serve in such a visible leadership role.

Most Bible dictionaries devote less than a paragraph to Ananias. Luke tells us only that he was a disciple and that the Lord spoke to him in a vision, commanding him to go to a street called Straight and to lay hands on a man named Saul that he might regain his sight.

But this Saul (later Paul) wasn't always a missionary! And Ananias was acquainted with him by reputation only. "Lord, I have heard from many people about this man, how much harm he has done to Your saints in Jerusalem" (v. 13). Further, he was

KINGDOM † PROMISES

aware that Saul had been given the authority to arrest all of those who would dare address Jesus as Lord. In other words, Ananias was being commanded to visit a man who had the authority to harass and arrest him for his faith in Christ.

Ananias's protest was cut short, however, by the adversative conjunction "but." The Lord spoke to him, explaining that he had chosen Saul to carry the name of Jesus before Gentiles, kings, and the sons of Israel. Paul had a large and visible kingdom assignment, a platform of opportunity to greatly expand the reach of the early church to the nations.

But we shouldn't forget the contribution of Ananias. Paul certainly didn't. He described Ananias as a "devout man according to the law, having a good reputation with all the Jews residing there" (Acts 22:12). In God's economy the obedience of Ananias to the Lord's divine interruption was of equal importance to the work of the great apostle. God wants each of us to fulfill our kingdom purpose. Most of us will never know, this side of glory, what kingdom role we have played.

BUT GOD
Exposes Our Prejudices

{ **Acts 10:28** But God has
shown me that I must not
call any person common
or unclean. }

Old habits die hard. And old habits
that are backed up by family or religious
tradition are even more difficult to put to
death. So when Peter was faced with a
command from the Lord that required him
to reassess his attitudes, God intervened
with a definitive "but."

Acts 10 opens with a simple statement:
"There was a man in Caesarea named
Cornelius." We're given quite a glowing
introduction to this Gentile man. He was a
centurion of the Italian Regiment, a devout
man who had done many charitable deeds
for the Jewish people and had even led his
entire household to fear God. The Lord
had sent an angelic messenger to tell him
that God had heard his prayers and that
he should call for Simon Peter.

Like a drama unfolding on two different stages, we discover that Peter was
meanwhile praying on his housetop at noon

and became hungry. Then God gave him a vision in which a large sheet was lowered from heaven, filled with four-footed animals, reptiles, and birds. A voice instructed him to eat. But Peter's upbringing told him that unclean animals must never be used for food. Peter objected three times, and the Lord responded, "What God has made clean, you must not call common" (v. 15).

Now the two scenes begin to merge. While Peter was pondering the meaning of this vision, the messengers from Cornelius arrived. And God told Peter to accompany them without reservation, "because I have sent them" (v. 20). It was an act forbidden by a Jew—to associate or visit with a foreigner, a person once thought to be "common or unclean."

This may on the surface seem like an insignificant event, but this heralded the beginning of the Gentile ministry. Now the early church was poised to take the good news to the nations. And we are reminded that an act of obedience we may consider to be of small import can truly have large kingdom impact—even in our own lives.

BUT GOD
Raised the Son

> **Acts 13:29–30** They took Him down from the tree and put Him in a tomb. But God raised Him from the dead.

This "But God" statement stands at the center of history. Everything in the Christian faith hangs on this great reversal. The crucifixion was the heart of Satan's strategy, but the resurrection was the profound answer of sovereign God.

The events surrounding the crucifixion were carried out by men who were mere pawns in the hands of God's adversary. Luke tells us that even though there were no grounds for the death penalty, the residents of Jerusalem and their rulers pressed for it because they did not comprehend the truth about Jesus, even though they had read about him every Sabbath.

These men in their ignorance had unwittingly become players in the drama which would fulfill the prophecies of how Jesus must suffer and die. Not only did they press for the death sentence, but death by crucifixion. Notice the description of the cross as "the tree." This term "tree" is used to underline the connection with Deuteronomy 21:23: "You are not to leave his corpse on the tree overnight but are to bury him that day, for anyone hung on a tree is under God's curse." Crucifixion was not only an excruciatingly painful and cruel way to die, it was an abomination for the Jews.

So when all was complete and the prophecies of his passion had been fulfilled, they took his dead body from the tree and put him in a tomb. (The mention of the tomb is intended to underline the reality of his death.) But God reversed the sentence of men and the work of the enemy.

This note of resurrection and triumph was a clear mark of early apostolic preaching. God raised Jesus from the dead, who then appeared to numerous people who could give witness to having seen the risen Lord. This historic event is of such magnitude, Paul would declare: "If Christ has not been raised, your faith is worthless; you are still in your sins" (1 Cor. 15:17). Aren't we glad that our Father interjected with a resounding "But God."

BUT GOD
Loves Us

> **Romans 5:8** But God proves His own love for us in that while we were still sinners Christ died for us!

Some images remain burned into your mind. You can call them back up with such detail and color, they seem to be a current event.

One such image for me is the picture of a secret service agent climbing onto the back of a black limousine and throwing himself over the body of a slumping, dying President Kennedy. It was an action that would prove to be "too little, too late," but nonetheless I was taken by the action of one man who was willing to lay down his life for another.

Romans 5 is one of my favorite chapters in all the Bible. It begins with one of the great "therefore" passages in Scripture—"Therefore, since we have been declared righteous by faith, we have peace with God through our Lord Jesus Christ" (v. 1). Paul, the author, went on to talk about our present access to God, which allows us to stand in grace and rejoice in the hope of his glory. Even our tribulations bring joy because we know that our hope cannot disappoint, since the love of God has been poured out in our hearts through the Holy Spirit.

But we sometimes forget that all of this came at a great price. "For while we were still helpless, at the appointed moment, Christ died for the ungodly" (v. 6). Paul reminded us, in fact, that rarely would someone die for a just person. In a rare case, yes, someone might offer his life to save a person he deemed to be just and good. But Christ died for us when we were still sinners.

The text places a unique emphasis on this act as proof of "God's own love"—love that is particular to God himself, the death of Christ being the ultimate manifestation of it. The phrase "while we were still sinners" parallels the similar "while we were still helpless" in verse 6. Christ's death was not prompted by any quality that made us deserving of such a gift. It stands as an absolute testimony to the great love of God for man.

BUT GOD
Chooses the Unworthy

{
1 Corinthians 1:27 (NASB)
But God has chosen the foolish
things of the world to shame
the wise.
}

Do you ever feel as though you are insignificant and unimportant? Do you ever wonder if your life will make a difference? When your pastor asks for someone to teach a class or lead a committee, do you think, "I'm just not worthy to serve God"?

For all of us who have ever felt like that, this great "But God" statement is a reassuring reminder.

Corinth was an interesting church, to say the least. There were members in their midst who had become spiritually arrogant as a result of possessing certain spiritual gifts. These super-spiritual members perhaps made many others in the church feel all the more inferior.

But Paul brought them back to reality by bringing up a stark comparison: "Brothers, consider your calling: not many are wise from a human perspective, not many powerful, not many of noble birth" (v. 26).

Viewed from the world's perspective, the early Christian movement was made up of very ordinary folks, just like us. Have you ever looked closely at the original twelve disciples? Fishermen, tax collectors, zealots—not a very auspicious group, yet they managed to turn the world upside down.

So, yes, if the early believers were being honest with themselves, they knew that very few of them were super talented or socially superior. Their worth had come purely from the fact that God had "chosen" them—a phrase Paul repeated three times in verses 27–28 alone. Those whom the world deemed to be foolish and weak were shown to be just the opposite by the choice of God.

These verses do not demean the Corinthians believers; rather, they exalt the sheer grace of God. When we have a clear understanding of who we are—including the enormity of our sin—we know how unworthy and insignificant we are in our human flesh. But the incredible good news is that God has chosen us in Christ through his redeeming love.

BUT GOD
Reveals His Love to Us

> **1 Corinthians 2:9–10 (NIV)** No mind has conceived what God has prepared for those who love Him, but God has revealed it.

I first discovered this verse when I was studying years ago in England. The Corinthian letter was central to my graduate work there, and this verse became one of my favorites.

Truly, the church at Corinth was anything but boring. As we saw in the previous reading, some of its members had become spiritually arrogant, boasting of their special wisdom and looking down upon Paul for his lack of wise teaching (as they saw it). But Paul spoke of a wisdom that cannot be comprehended by natural ability, and this is the context in which this incredible promise is found.

It appears to be based on a rather loose citation of Isaiah 64:4. Note that neither eye, nor ear, nor heart can comprehend what "God has prepared for those who love Him" (v. 9). To Paul's original reader, the heart was not so much the seat of emotion

as it was the center of his entire being —
his thought, will, and emotion. So when
Paul combined the heart with the eye and
ear, he was declaring that none of our
human faculties could fully grasp God's
power and provision for his people.

But because we cannot understand this
on our own, God has done something
extraordinarily gracious — he has chosen to
reveal it to us. The things we believers
know about the goodness and love of God
are not truths we've figured out. We know
them not because of skill, cunning, intel-
lect, or special wisdom, but because God
has been willing to reveal them to us by his
Holy Spirit, who "searches everything,
even the deep things of God" (v. 10).

Stop a moment and mediate on this.
The phrase "what God has prepared"
indicates that there is nothing haphazard
about his abundant provision. It is based
on God's purpose and has flowed from the
cross at great expense.

And we are the humble recipients of
this grace. Thank the Father for his abundant provision and his desire to make it
known to you.

BUT GOD
Does the Work

> **1 Corinthians 3:6** I planted, Apollos watered, but God gave the growth.

It is easy for us to put our focus on people, even in the church. Sometimes the pastor receives the credit for the church's growth; sometimes he gets the blame for the lack of it. The early Christians in Corinth fell prey to this same tendency. Some wanted to claim that they were in Paul's camp, while others claimed Apollos as their spiritual leader. This had resulted in envy and strife and had led to division in the church.

In response Paul asked and answered a very pointed question—"So, what is Apollos? And what is Paul? They are servants through whom you believed, and each has the role the Lord has given" (v. 5). God had used both of them to bring about the conversion of various members of the church in Corinth by his grace, mercy, and calling. But all authentic spiritual work is accomplished by God. This was the crucial point Paul was trying to underline in this part of his epistle.

He likened the process to agriculture. Paul had arrived first and had planted the seed of the gospel. Apollos came along and watered that seed. But it was God who was actually accomplishing the growth. (The verbs that speak of planting and watering are in the aorist tense in the Greek, indicating a specific point in time. The verb translated "gave the growth," though, is imperfect, indicating that it is a continuous action.)

We can take several lessons from this passage: *First, keep spiritual leaders in the proper perspective.* We can and should appreciate them, but not worship or cling to them. They are simply vessels through whom God works. *Second, Paul and Apollos had different roles, but God used each of them.* Every pastor and church leader is uniquely gifted, but God himself is the one who creates such diversity. *Third, God works through gifted servants.* This doesn't belittle anyone. It is a glorious thought that God desires to accomplish his work through us.

BUT GOD
Has Uniquely Designed Us

> **1 Corinthians 12:18** But now God has placed the parts, each one of them, in the body just as He wanted.

Have you ever felt like you just didn't belong? It's easy to become intimidated when we see someone who appears to be uniquely gifted and talented. When we compare ourselves with them through our own eyes, we are the "Weakest Link!"

Over the last several pages we have looked at passages originally written to the church at Corinth. Some of the members of that church had allowed their giftedness to cause them to become spiritually arrogant. This in turn had caused others to have a diminished view of their own spiritual worth.

Both of these conditions—over-evaluation and under-evaluation—have a negative impact on the kingdom potential of the believer and the church. But Paul had an intriguing and somewhat humorous way to combat this problem. He pictured a scene where human body parts were having an argument about their relative rank and importance. For example, "If the foot should say, 'Because I am not a hand, I don't belong to the body,' in spite of this it still belongs to the body" (v. 15). Then in equally humorous fashion, he pondered what the body would be like if the whole body were an eye or an ear.

Two points are clearly established using this analogy. Each body part has its own unique function. The body requires diversity to function properly. But beyond this is another profound truth that cannot be overlooked: God designed the human body as he wanted. The members of the body are not stuck together in a haphazard fashion. They are individually and intentionally placed together by God. His design and care doesn't just extend to those who appear to have the more spectacular gifts. He cares equally for every member of the body.

Therefore, you are special simply because you were designed by God with purpose. You were created by him, redeemed by his grace, gifted and empowered by his Spirit, enabling you to join him in advancing his kingdom. Make it your goal to discover your God-given place in the body and thus please your Creator.

BUT GOD
Comforts Us

> **2 Corinthians 7:6** But God,
> who comforts the humble,
> comforted us.

One of the things that attracts us to the apostle Paul is his openness and honesty. He often drew aside the curtain and allowed us to see both his pain and his joy. Paul's missionary journeys were fraught with challenges. He spoke of shipwrecks, imprisonment, beatings, hard labor, and a lack of sufficient food and clothing. But his greatest concern was for the "daily pressure" exerted on him by his "care for all the churches" (2 Cor. 11:28).

It wasn't easy being Paul.

In the verse preceding today's assurance of divine comfort and intervention, Paul mentioned what had happened to him during one of his missionary visits. "When we came into Macedonia, we had no rest. Instead, we were afflicted in every way: struggles on the outside, fears inside." In some way, I suppose, it is encouraging to discover that the great apostle experienced the same feelings and concerns we do. "Struggles on the outside" probably referred to his physical challenges and conflicts with unbelievers, while "fears inside" referred to his concern for his converts. If you have read the Corinthian letters, you are aware that some of the people Paul had ministered to actually turned against him. Have you ever had a similar experience either with a friend or family member? You can understand, then, how emotional suffering can often have a far greater impact on us than physical suffering can.

The good news, though, is that God is "the God of all comfort" (2 Cor. 1:3), who had personally comforted Paul by the coming of his companion Titus. We sometimes miss God's comfort because we fail to see his ministering hand in the everyday visitors he sends our way. Titus himself had been comforted and encouraged by the Corinthians, and he conveyed this message to Paul, which cheered him in his difficult time. Have you been comforted by a messenger recently? Have you been the messenger of comfort for someone else?

BUT GOD
Shows Mercy

> **Philippians 2:27 (NASB)**
> Indeed he was sick to the
> point of death, but God
> had mercy on him.

Paul wrote to his beloved church in Philippi from prison, where he had received assistance from them and wanted to return the favor. Thus he had decided to send Timothy to them as soon as possible. This young pastor would be able to give them word about him, as well as come back with an update to keep Paul encouraged. Yet the circumstances of his imprisonment had caused Paul to delay sending him.

He assured the Philippians, though, that Timothy's delay would not affect his sending of Epaphroditus, a man whose name meant "charming" or "amiable." He, in fact, had been the messenger to Paul from the Philippian church, bearing their gift of support. "I am fully supplied," Paul wrote back, "having received from Epaphroditus what you provided—a fragrant offering, a welcome sacrifice, pleasing to God" (Phil. 4:18).

Epaphroditus had greatly endeared himself to the apostle. His presence alone had far exceeded any financial gift he had brought on behalf of the church. Paul described him as his brother, his co-worker, his fellow-soldier.

But Epaphroditus had apparently fallen gravely ill, either on his way to see Paul or during his stay. "He came close to death for the work of Christ, risking his life to make up what was lacking in your ministry to me" (2:30). Epaphroditus was filled with emotion for the concern his illness had created in his home church.

Once again, however, the kingdom perspective is indicated by a "But God." The Lord had mercy on Epaphroditus. Yet there is a second "but" statement that occurs in the same sentence. God not only had mercy on his seriously ill servant, "but also on me"—on Paul—"so that I would not have one grief on top of another." God's mercy in the healing of Epaphroditus was simultaneously a gift of mercy to Paul.

Have you thanked God lately for the mercy he has demonstrated to you . . . by way of his ministry to someone you love?

BUT GOD
Cannot Be Restrained

> **2 Timothy 2:9** For this I suffer, to the point of being bound like a criminal; but God's message is not bound.

The impact of Paul's second letter to Timothy becomes all the more powerful when we recall that Paul wrote it from prison while contemplating his own death. Yet in spite of his circumstances, these letters contain a message of sure victory, not only for the original readers but for all the young Timothys of every generation.

Paul used various images and analogies (such as the military, athletics, and farming) to encourage Timothy's faithfulness to his calling and work as a pastor. These were good teaching tools that helped him remember and apply Paul's lessons. Ultimately, however, Paul clearly directed Timothy to keep his mind focused on the powerful gospel of the resurrection.

After all, this is what it was all about for Paul, just as it is for us. His bold proclamation of the gospel and the disturbance his preaching created were the basis for the charges against him, charges that now had him "bound" like a common criminal. (It is noteworthy that the only other place where this word is used in the New Testament is in Luke 23, where it describes the men crucified with Jesus.)

Yet the contrast declared in his "but God" statement is stark and powerful. Yes, Paul himself may have been "bound like a criminal," but the gospel was certainly not.

One reason this was true was because others were openly and freely declaring the gospel, even with Paul in chains. But it also had another, more subtle implication—that the gospel Paul had declared prior to his imprisonment was still having an impact. The Spirit was still using Paul's words to draw souls to salvation.

Once the gospel is declared, it continues to have power. You will never know the impact of your life and ministry until you get to heaven. There will be people you will meet again that you have shared with and ministered to—some who may have spurned and rejected you on earth—but who are now in heaven for this reason: the gospel cannot be bound.

BUT GOD
Stands with Us

2 Timothy 4:17 But the Lord stood with me and strengthened me, so that the proclamation might be fully made through me.

Have you ever been in a situation where you had to stand alone? It isn't a very comfortable feeling. But Paul discovered that even when everyone else had deserted him, he was not standing alone.

In this final section of his second letter to Timothy, Paul appealed to him to "make every effort to come to me soon" (v. 9). It is obvious that Paul was feeling somewhat deserted. In fact, he listed the names of several who had left him. Some had probably left rather quietly, armed with their own excuses. Others, like Alexander the coppersmith, had left in a blaze of glory, doing "great harm" to Paul in the process (v. 14). With some sadness he noted, "Only Luke is with me" (v. 11).

In verse 16, Paul referred to his "first defense," apparently a preliminary investigation that preceded a formal trial, where "no one came to my assistance." He doesn't seem to say this with bitterness, but rather to bring into sharper relief the impact of divine assistance on his life.

With strong resolve he declared: "But the Lord stood with me and strengthened me." The Lord gave him great moral courage, which enabled him not only to defend his own case but also to ensure that the Gentiles continued to hear the gospel.

When Paul introduced himself to the recipients of the letter to the Romans, he made a similar statement: "We have received grace and apostleship through Him to bring about the obedience of faith among all the nations, on behalf of His name" (Rom. 1:5). God's desire has always been that every nation hear the gospel. So Paul not only celebrated God's personal plan for his life but also the opportunity afforded him to preach in the official center of Rome. The kingdom person looks at every event in terms of kingdom possibility.

When you feel that you are standing alone, know that the Lord will stand with you and strengthen you. Ask him to help you see every moment in terms of its kingdom potential.

BUT GOD
Corrects Us for Our Good

> **Hebrews 12:10** They disciplined us for a short time based on what seemed good to them, but He does it for our benefit.

"This hurts me worse than it does you, son!"

"I'm doing this for your good!"

"One day you'll thank me for this!"

I can still hear vividly some of the things my dad used to tell me, right before he would discipline me. I must confess, at the time I found them hard to believe. As time progressed, though, and I accepted the responsibility of being a father, I came to appreciate my dad's discipline.

If you are a believer, you've experienced the discipline of the Lord as he has brought correction and reproof. For that reason it would be worth your time to read all of Hebrews 12. The writer reminded us that God calls us his children and that we should not take that privilege lightly. Only in the context of our sonship can we understand the Lord's discipline as an act of great love for his children.

The writer of Hebrews then compared God's perfect parenting skills to those of earthly, fallible parents. Their discipline is for a brief period, based on what seems best at the time. But every parent would admit that they've made mistakes while disciplining their children. Sometimes we discipline from anger or embarrassment. At other times we act without all the facts.

But the good news is, God disciplines us "for our benefit." God is perfect in character, and therefore his discipline flows from that perfection. Even when we don't fully understand it, we can rely on the fact that God in his perfect wisdom and love can never impose discipline on us that is not in our best interest. Remember, he created us and knows us better than we know ourselves.

We sometimes misunderstand God's discipline because we lose sight of his ultimate desire for his children—"so that we can share his holiness." God disciplines us so that we continually become more like him. When we understand this precious truth, we will welcome God's discipline as a gift more precious than gold.

BUT GOD
Keeps Giving Us Grace

> **James 4:6** But He gives greater grace. Therefore He says, "God resists the proud, but gives grace to the humble."

Do you ever feel like you are being torn in two? Paul once talked about his struggle with fleshly desires and his desire to obey God's laws in terms of an agonizing battle (see Romans 7:7–25). He spoke of needing rescue from this body of death.

James spoke of the same spiritual struggle in slightly different terms, but the solution and the resolution are the same in each case.

In verse 4 James warned against spiritual adultery. A familiar Old Testament idea is that Jehovah is the "husband" of his people (Isa. 54:5). There are two rivals for our love and allegiance—God and the world. When we choose worldly pleasure as the chief end of our life, we become enemies of God. Paul spoke of a time when men would be tempted to be "lovers of pleasure rather than lovers of God" (2 Tim. 3:4–5).

But the Spirit of God who dwells within us yearns for us jealously. Have you ever thought that the Spirit of God yearns over you with such intensity? With jealous envy? This is not the kind of jealousy we normally think of, tinged with pride and selfishness. His jealousy is pure and altogether holy.

Yet the goal of possessing unrivaled loyalty and devotion to God is a lofty one indeed, and therefore we are encouraged to know that "he gives greater grace." The Holy Spirit who longs for us with pure passion supplies an even more abundant supply of grace in order that we can attain the goal of complete surrender. Such knowledge of God's great love for us puts to death pride and leads to a biblical sense of humility.

When I think that God loved me so much that he sent his Son to die in my place, I am overwhelmed with gratitude. When I think that his Holy Spirit indwells me and loves me with such intensity that he is jealous for my affection, I am humbled and awed. It should cause us to respond with obedience and unalloyed affection.

Appendix

The promises of this book are based on one's relationship to Christ. If you have not yet entered a personal relationship with Jesus Christ, I encourage you to make this wonderful discovery today. I like to use the very simple acrostic—LIFE—to explain this, knowing that God wants you not only to inherit *eternal* life but also to experience *earthly* life to its fullest.

L = LOVE
It all begins with God's love. God created you in his image. This means you were created to live in relationship with him. *"For God loved the world in this way: He gave His One and Only Son, so that everyone who believes in Him will not perish but have eternal life" (John 3:16)*

But if God loves you and desires a relationship with you, why do you feel so isolated from him?

I = ISOLATION
This isolation is created by our sin—our rebellion against God—which separates us from him and from others. *"For all have sinned and fall short of the glory of God"* (Rom. 3:23). *"For the wages of sin is death, but the gift of God is eternal life in Christ Jesus our Lord"* (Rom. 6:23).

You might wonder how you can overcome this isolation and have an intimate relationship with God.

F = FORGIVENESS
The only solution to man's isolation and separation from a holy God is forgiveness. *"For Christ also suffered for sins once for all, the righteous for the unrighteous, that He might bring you to God, after being put to death in the fleshly realm but made alive in the spiritual realm"* (1 Peter 3:18).

The only way our relationship can be restored with God is through the forgiveness of our sins. Jesus Christ died on the cross for this very purpose.

E = Eternal Life
You can have full and abundant life in this present life . . . and eternal life when you die. *"But to all who did receive Him, He gave them the right to be children of God, to those who believe in His name"* (John 1:12). *"A thief comes only to steal and to kill and to destroy. I have come that they may have life and have it in abundance"* (John 10:10).

Is there any reason you wouldn't like to have a personal relationship with God?

THE PLAN OF SALVATION

It's as simple as ABC. All you have to do is:

A = Admit you are a sinner. Turn from your sin and turn to God. *"Repent and turn back, that your sins may be wiped out so that seasons of refreshing may come from the presence of the Lord"* (Acts 3:19).

B = Believe that Jesus died for your sins and rose from the dead enabling you to have life. *"I have written these things to you who believe in the name of the Son of God, so that you may know that you have eternal life"* (1 John 5:13).

C = Confess verbally and publicly your belief in Jesus Christ. *"If you confess with your mouth, 'Jesus is Lord,' and believe in your heart that God raised Him from the dead, you will be saved. With the heart one believes, resulting in righteousness, and with the mouth one confesses, resulting in salvation"* (Rom. 10:9–10).

You can invite Jesus Christ to come into your life right now. Pray something like this:

"God, I admit that I am a sinner. I believe that you sent Jesus, who died on the cross and rose from the dead, paying the penalty for my sins. I am asking that you forgive me of my sin, and I receive your gift of eternal life. It is in Jesus' name that I ask for this gift. Amen."

Signed _____

Date _____

If you have a friend or family member who is a Christian, tell them about your decision. Then find a church that teaches the Bible, and let them help you go deeper with Christ.

KINGDOM PROMISES

If you've enjoyed this book of Kingdom
Promises, you may want to consider
reading one of the others in the series:

 We Are
0-8054-2781-3

 We Can
0-8054-2780-5

 But God
0-8054-2782-1

 He Is
0-8054-2783-X

Available in stores nationwide and through
major online retailers. For a complete look
at Ken Hemphill titles, make sure to visit
broadmanholman.com/hemphill.